GOD, SEX, and MUSICAL THEATRE

meditations for unlocking the powerful self

Kristin Hanggi

Copyright © Kristin Hanggi, 2020

All rights reserved. No part of this book may be used, performed, or reproduced in any manner whatsoever without written permission from the publisher except in the case of brief quotations embodied in critical articles or reviews.

First edition.
ISBN: 978-1949342284

Cover Design by Luna aït Oumeghar
Interior Layout by Winona León
Interior Illustrations by Brent French
Edited by Wess Mongo Jolley, Aly Sarafa, and Derrick C Brown
Proofread by Wess Mongo Jolley
Author Photo by Jennifer Castle

Birch Bench Press

*To the women who have been silencing their desire to get to goodness,
may this book be your reminder that your good is in your desire.
There is nothing to prove. You were born whole.
The world needs your radiance.*

"All we really want to do is dance." — Joseph Campbell

GOD, SEX, *and* MUSICAL THEATRE

GOD, SEX, and MUSICAL THEATRE

CONJURING

God, Sex, and Musical Theatre 11
Road Map 17
Three Incantations for My Heart 23
A Prayer 26
What Washes Away 27
The Unknown 31
My Real Job 34

INITIATION

Life in Pieces 41
Dating 46
Rise 49
Crucible 52
Mercurial 57
The Body Knows 59
Four Incantations for My Sacral Chakra 61
Affaire d'Honneur, or The Hook Up 69
Half the Battle 72

ATHAME

The Important Things 77
Me and Tennessee 78
Download This 82
Magic Lessons 87
Pyrotechnics 89
Seek First 93
A New Friend 97
And Then She Said 100
Grow Ourselves Beautiful 105
Coaxing 107

THE GOLDEN ELIXIR

Love Is Here 113
An Affair to Remember 117
A New Way of Seeing 118
Invitation 119
Love High 125
Regeneration 127
Story Tellers 133
That Flower Next 136

Acknowledgments 141

CONJURING

GOD, SEX, AND MUSICAL THEATRE

One day, in grad school, my writing professor turned to the entire class and said, *"Have you ever noticed that all of Kristin's work is about sex?"*

I remember I felt humiliated — exposed and guilty.
I also think I *was* sleeping with someone in that class.
Jay, I believe his name was.

I haven't thought about Jay in 20 years —
his epic shoulders, his intense masculinity, his
cute jock-like awkwardness with me —
But I *have* thought about that professor's comment.

Often.

It felt like a violation.

Why did he feel like it was okay to point out the sexuality of my work to the class? What was the point of that? Was he trying to shame me? Or is that *my* shame I feel? Do I feel embarrassed by how sexual I am?

That comment has stuck with me, coming back to me again and again, And I admit to myself: "Yes, I *am* interested in sex."

Why is that? Why do I want to talk about it? And talk about how we do it, and our feelings about it? Why do I want to talk about *my* feelings about it? Why am I so fascinated by how it can be fun and intimate and painful?

Maybe it's because it can reveal *us* to *ourselves*.

In accepting our sexuality, we also have to accept ourselves.

When I was in kindergarten, all I wanted to do at recess was play The Kissing Game. Have you played? Just like tag, except it ends in something much better than being "It." I've never been a fast runner but kissing gives me lightning speed.

You and me, Davy Kay, we're gonna kiss.

That desire hasn't gone away. I still want to play with the boys and
kiss them — or have them kiss me. I also find that I'm open
to it being a girl or a boy. I just think kissing is awesome
and I wonder why we *all* don't do it *all* the time.

I've always had this big, powerful sexuality in me —
as long as I can remember. Bold, audacious, and confident.
I always felt I had to keep a lid on it, keep it hidden.
It felt bigger than me, and there's always been this terror
that it was going to get me into trouble.

You know what else I used to love as a little kid?

    Jesus.

I felt my body get filled up with light when I would sing songs
to a power that I did not understand. I liked to memorize Bible
verses because afterwards they would give me chocolate.

There were a lot of great things about church.

I remember talking to angels as a small girl.
I remember feeling connected to unseen forces.

One of my earliest memories was looking out my family's backseat
car window and thinking,

it's so weird that everyone is in bodies,
moving around, pretending that this life thing is real.

I also think I felt a certain solace. A comfort. A love.
It was always with me. And it *was* me.

And so, two things were present in me as a small child, that are
explicitly still here — as bright and as bold as ever:

    I love God.
    I love Sex.

I also think it's interesting that many people are
scared of God, or talking about God.
And many people are scared of sex.

Maybe it's because they are private things.

Your beliefs about there being a Divine presence in the world (or not)
feels very personal. And who you have sex with (and how)
is also very personal.

Maybe that's why I like them both.

I want to talk about the deepest things. I want to go inside to the stuff that
seems scary and too close and ask, "what's here?" And I really want to give
myself permission to believe what I believe, and have sex the way I want to. I
want to give that permission to myself, and to others.

And then I want to make a musical about it.
I direct musicals, if you don't know.

So, let me amend my above statement and say:

> I love God.
> I love Sex.
> I love Musical Theatre.

I often feel embarrassed and shy about how much I love the Divine.
I also feel embarrassed and shy about how much I love sex.
Frankly, I probably feel embarrassed and shy about
how much I love musical theatre.
Or that I even write poetry to begin with.

But I'm starting to wonder if real self-love is about embracing
what we love. Even if it doesn't make sense. Maybe the only
thing that's important is that we accept it.

Through loving what we love, we begin to know ourselves.

It could be that what I love is transcendence. The reaching for
the sacred. The desire for the moments in life that feel *holy*.

> That's how I feel when I kiss.
> That's how I feel when I pray.
> That's how I feel when the lights go down in a theater.

My friend Mikey said to me, "Musical theatre? Isn't that just the combination of God and sex?"

And I thought, "It *is* — when it's really good."

ROAD MAP

My mother used to say that kids don't come *from* you,
they come *through* you. All parents at some time
have to learn the art of letting go. A lesson in loving
someone so much you say: *You get to decide.*

That's how the Universe loves us.

It's like we've been handed this ancient road map
with the instructions written on top in script.
It reads (hear the dramatic theme music swelling
in the background): *Take whatever path you choose.*

Now, I know many of us wish our map
had come highlighted (like Triple-A used to do it)
or turn-by-turn (like the iPhone directs)
because then we'd know which road to take.

We wouldn't get lost, drive off the trail, or (if you're
anything like me) crash head-first into a petrified tree
going 80 miles an hour, just so that you can look up
and say, *Wow, that didn't work now, did it?*

But there's a definition of love that means freedom.
It means *go how you wanna go.*

And, guess what? It's all valuable. Every route is scenic.
Wherever you go, there you are. And there is a really
good place to be. Because there's knowledge there.
And you're able, at any moment, to pull over at a rest
stop, eat some trail mix, take a breath, then try a different
route.

Because check it out, behind my shoulder, see that? That's
my past.

I know. I can see the damage from here too.

But after eavesdropping on the conversations
of old truck drivers who've been doing this a lot
longer than I have, this is what I've
learned: *Back there doesn't drive me.*

Nope. That road behind me has nothing to do with where I'm going.
The engine — my engine — is alive here and now. My future has everything
to do with the direction I'm pointed. And the road I just traveled
should never be discounted because it got me right here.
No mistake.

All roads eventually lead to the same place and
sometimes getting lost is an important part
of figuring out which way you want to go.

Now, looking back with new eyes, I see
for the first time, not the collisions, but that the line
down the middle of the road I took was golden.
My path, even when I couldn't see it, was holy.

As I face ahead, I know where
I'm going is where I'm being led.
See, I got smart.
I hired a driver.
And we're gonna co-pilot this trip together.
She's a bad ass.
She's sexy.
And she wears a lot of leather.

In a voice that sounds like smooth jazz, she says to me,
Sit back, baby, put your feet up, turn the air on, and relax.
You can look out the window and let me drive,
and I'll take you places you never thought you could go,
more awesome than you ever dreamed of.

Of course, being the control-freak that I am, I keep
wanting to grab the wheel, put my foot on the brake, or check
the engine lights on the dashboard, just to make sure
she hasn't missed anything. And anytime I try to
over-manage out of fear and doubt (sending us

careening into the bushes again) she just laughs.
Is that really where you want to go?

See, the thing about this driver is that she loves me.
She lets me choose.
I hand back the controls.
All right, navigate.
I am learning the art of letting go.
That's my choice.

My driver leans over. *You can trust me,*
she whispers, *but you might want to put your seatbelt on.*
I know a secret route, and honey, this drive
is about to blow your mind.

I breathe in, look down at my map: all roads have become
one road, stretching off the page and into the unknown.

I buckle up.

Oh, let me give you my card,
she adds. *If anyone asks,*
you can tell them that I work for free.

Now, let's enjoy this ride.

They say that
the door to liberation
swings inward,
and waiting
in the home of your heart
is a Tough Ass Mother
who wants to shake
the world to its core.

THREE INCANTATIONS FOR MY HEART

i.

What most people don't know about hearts
is that if you used the world's most powerful microscope
and looked in on those ventricles pumping away like crazy,
you would find, under a small valve in the aorta,
in the center of every heart,
is a perfect gold compass.

But instead of north, south, east, and west,
it only has two directions:
"Who you really are" and "Everything else."
That's why, when you're living someone else's life,
even if you try to pretend it doesn't bother you,
your heart knows the difference.

ii.

I used to live my life straight out of my heart like a slingshot.
I was breaking through windows, shattering glass
because I liked the sound and the size of the impact.
Until I stepped back and realized what a mess I'd made.

See, after a while, too many splintered shards
got caught in the middle of my chest,
and so I did the only reasonable thing:
I sent my heart off to be fixed.

I stay away from windows lately. Nothing breaks
if I play it safe. And safe makes sense.

Except…
That's not me.
I am mischievous.
I am unafraid.
I am a fly-by-night, anything-could-happen, unpredictable,

slingshot adventurer of the Soul.
And that's why magic follows me.

So, I sent my heart to the repair shop.

I went and picked her up last Tuesday. I thought she looked
better than ever, maybe even a little sexier with a scar or two.

Immediately, my heart wanted to get back to
the business of playing it unsafe.

iii.

Logically, it was only a matter of time
before my head staged an intervention with my heart.
It won't let her betray me again, making another bad choice.
My head declared things were better — more regulated —
when it was in charge. Graciously, my newly repaired heart
offered to go away on a permanent vacation.

Of course, it was a vacation on a secret island
somewhere off the coast of Brazil
where everyone likes to sing songs about whimsy
and rainbows, eat mint-chip ice cream for dinner,
and paint exotic flowers on their bedroom walls.

Meanwhile, my head keeps a very tight schedule.
And counts calories. And goes to Pilates.

And after a couple of days of acting reasonably
I really miss the sound of my too-loud laugh,
or the exhilaration I get from a little well-crafted naughtiness.
I even miss crying in the shower where my tears blend in
and nobody knows but me.

I want my heart to come back.

I make a long-distance call to my heart and tell her so…
And, after my request, she says, "Kristin, I've been liberated! Why
would I want to come back there and get locked up again?"

"It's not that bad," I tell my heart, masking my obvious desperation.
"We just have a few new rules — safety rules — that we follow."

"No," my heart replies, stubbornly. "I know how it is!
Your head is always trying to get us to go to bed early,
eat reasonable portions of dessert, not fall in love too quickly,
and keep our feet from dancing in line at public places!
That's not the life I want to live!"

"Well, you know, it's not me…" I protest, vigorously.
"I *want* to do those things. But my head makes a good point:
everyone else wouldn't understand. Other people would get scared
by that kind of freedom, it would make them uncomfortable."

"I know," says my heart, a little sadly. "That's why I'm not free."

"So, what do we do?" My head interrupts, thoroughly exasperated.
(I didn't even know my head was on the line!)
"Just let *you* run the place? You would go wild and make impetuous
decisions. Telling people exactly what you think, doing whatever you
want to do, and never considering the consequences. That sounds like a
mess! We could become homeless, lose all our friends, and be left alone!"

"Or…" says my heart, in the most tender of voices. "Every day could be a
series of made-up songs, silly dances, and intimate conversations with
strangers. And I would teach you the hidden ways of charm, show you
doors to worlds untraveled, and how you can wrap the sunset and put it in
your pocket. Now, I'm not saying, we won't accidentally take the wrong
road sometimes. And, it's true, in my enthusiasm, we could fall into a
ditch and have to climb our way out. But we must be willing
to take the risk."

I must admit, my heart drives a hard bargain.

"You're very dangerous," I whisper to her. "You push me
to the limit every time."

My heart replies, "I am a compass. All I do is point."

A PRAYER

Forces from above,
that encircle us and hold us:

I need help that isn't on this plane.
I really need something bigger than me to intercede.

Teach me.

Forces from above:
What do you want me to see right now?
I know that you are here.

And I must let go
to allow you to do your magic.

Help. Help.
Come down.

I will hold space for you because I have nothing else.
There is nothing more for me
than to create a space where you can enter.

WHAT WASHES AWAY

Yesterday I got caught in such a fear storm.
Feelings banging around in my body
thoughts a jumbled hurricane of "what if"
ripping apart my peace and drowning me
in a sea of *absolutely-not-here*.

It came and passed.

With it, something inside of me was washed away.

I'm being asked to let go of outcomes.
And I'm watching myself cling to them like a life boat.
I want something to keep me safe and dry.
The promise of a Promised Land.
Life says, "Nope, baby, I'm teaching you to swim."

Speaking my fears aloud is a lesson in buoyancy. Can I stay with myself when I'm scared, when my mind gets loud and full of judgement, without trying to fix anything, without apology? Can I go through my human pain, my floundering, with great empathy? I'm saving myself with my compassion for myself.

When I let go, I float.

Thank you, Kristin, for being brave. Isn't that the real lifesaver when the seas get unkind?

To see my honesty as bravery.
To weather the discomfort.
To be with myself in the process of the dark, rough nights.

Maybe the storm has its own joy.

It's teaching me to clear my mind more.
It's teaching me the power of presence.
It's teaching me that even if I think I see clouds approaching, inside of me, there's a place that can't be touched.

My safety is within.
And when I rest there
I am always safe.

When I know the stillness
I can head into the unknown.

Maybe that is walking on water?

The storm washes away all that is not us
so we can know the place within that no storm can touch.

The storm directs us to the places inside that are immoveable.

The storm teaches us who we are.

I'm learning
to allow life
to have its way
with me.

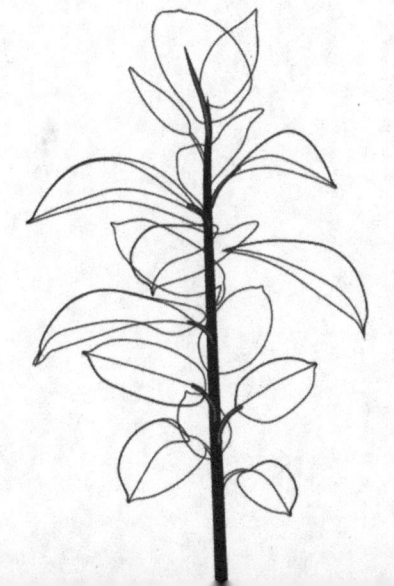

THE UNKNOWN

i.

AHHHHHHHH!!!!!

Sometimes I just wanna SCREAM!!!
I DON'T KNOW WHAT I'M DOING!!!!
I don't know what I'm doing.
I really don't.
But shit, you know what?
There's something Divine in me and it knows.
And that may sound silly to you
That's okay.
I have proof.

ii.

The Lyft driver who took me to the airport yesterday morning at 6:30 a.m. told me, unprompted, that the Universe will handle most of the work. I just gotta show up and trust what comes through me and that I will be given what I need, when I need it.
And then he hugged me after he took my bags.

If that's the kind of world I live in, one where there are angel Lyft drivers at the break of dawn, maybe I don't ever need to worry. Maybe I can just rest.

And I know that all I can do is be okay with not knowing.
I am taken care of.
I am taken care of.
This situation I'm dealing with is being taken care of.

iii.

I left my laptop in a New York City cab, along with the hard drive containing the only copy of a movie I had just shot. A week later, I received a call from an NYC employee who worked at 311 Lost and Found. A woman named Grace — yes, that was her name! — told me she had been put there by God to return my belongings to me, and that God wanted me to know that my faith could get bigger.

That's the kind of world I live in. Where angels work for New York City and call to give me messages from above and return my laptop.

I know people think I'm goofy. And that I believe in magic and unicorns and rainbows and elves.

I don't believe in elves.

But Divine Magic is always carrying me, so it's hard not to believe in it.

iv.

Right now, at this very moment, I feel fear banging around on the inside of my heart. I'm in a place that feels like a big old mess. And I don't know what to do.

There's something going on in my romantic relationship. He's hurting and there is rage. And I'm scared. We can't communicate with each other. So, either this is coming to a close, or it is transforming into something new. I want to believe there's a blessing here somewhere, but right now, it feels like tremendous grief. There is something happening here that I can't control. I can't control it. And I want to have faith at the same time.

And something is going on in my financial life. This year, the bottom has been falling out of all my projects. What I've done before isn't working. It's like the Divine is trying to redirect me to a new place. And I'm not sure what to do. I'm scared. And I want to have faith at the same time.

In my self-pitying moments, it all leaves me wanting to shake my fists at the heavens and say, "What am I doing wrong?"

I know, of course, this is not the question.
Life is asking me to ask different.

v.

Last night my dear friend came to my house and carried my
heavy suitcase up three flights of stairs. He bought me a
delicious dinner and he refused to let me pay. And he
asked me, "What are the empowering questions that
the Infinite is wanting you to ask?" And then he
did my dishes and offered me a foot rub.
I kid you not. Magic.

I sit with that this morning:
Who does love want me to be in this situation?
What abundance wants to come through me?
How do these qualities which are always within me
want to transform my life?

I'm listening.
Let my perception be open.
Let my heart be open.
Let me trust the path of the unknown.

MY REAL JOB

> *"The Master does his job*
> *and then stops.*
> *He understands that the universe*
> *is forever out of control,*
> *and that trying to dominate events*
> *goes against the current of the Tao.*
> *Because he believes in himself,*
> *he doesn't try to convince others.*
> *Because he is content with himself,*
> *he doesn't need others' approval.*
> *Because he accepts himself,*
> *the whole world accepts him."*
> — Verse 30, Tao Te Ching

Today my job is to accept myself.

I have a fantastic imagination, and my fantasy version of myself has rainbow hair and farts sparkles. She flies through sunsets, and looks great in a neon-colored unitard. She's highly entertaining. You would love her.

And my real self is… human.
A work in progress.
A work that never finishes.

And it's so nice to just put something pretty in a frame and say "done," right? It's so fulfilling when the curtain rises on opening night. It's so complete when the movie is released.

But you know what? You never really feel done then *either*. The artist knows there is always more work to do. The divine dissatisfaction that Martha Graham talks about is there, whispering to us that more of this story wants to be told.

So, my job today is not to judge myself—
the unique piece of art that I am.
But to love myself.
Where I am right now.
And all the potential in me.

If I'm willing to accept myself as I am, I can find my way to
appreciation. If I look in the mirror and see the way my eyes light up
when I'm thinking mischievous thoughts… I start to notice that I'm fun.
Silly. Beautiful. Inspiring. Creative.

She sneaks up on me.
My very own spirit sneaks up on me.

She's messy. And imperfect. And complicated.
And doing it one day at a time.
One day at a time is my job.

My job today is to release convincing others.
My job today is to release needing their approval.
My job today is to pray: *"Show me my job today."*

Job Description for myself:
Keep the Divine as my center. Stay connected to the truth of my being. Rest.
Play. Create my sacred work. Communicate & acknowledge my desires.
Take care of myself. Eat deliciously. Move. Sleep. Self-care. Art for my
Soul. Nurture my relationships. Allow my living environment to be a temple.
Discard what no longer brings me joy so I can make room for the new.
Create order. Tell the truth, especially when it's uncomfortable.
Be a good steward to my finances. Dream. Go on adventures. Forgive.
Keep learning. See everything as a blessing. Be available to what I don't know.
Hold a vision of a greater good. Stay in the wonder. Love.

I do my job.
I forget my job.
And I do my job again.

Then all I have to do is stop.
And let go.

I can never get enough of my love.

INITIATION

INITIATION

LIFE IN PIECES

Sometimes life gives you a metaphor so big, you can't miss it.
Life gave me a mother fucking couch.

My relationship of three years just got ripped apart at the seams:
no closure, no happy ending, nothing neat or tidy. Everything in pieces.
I look to the Divine and I say very clearly, "Tell me what to do."

And that's when I got a couch.

My dear friend offers me his very big and very expensive couch. For free.
All I have to do is move it. And when you suddenly find yourself with
your evenings available, the idea of a big, comfy couch for cuddling with
your cat sounds… Well, it sounds a little depressing, but let's just say
it will get some use.

So, I call the moving company, and learn it's pretty affordable to move a
couch across town. That's a win!

Saturday, I show up at my friend's apartment a few minutes before 7 a.m.
and the movers are already there. They wrap up the gigantic couch,
haul it into their van, and drive it a few blocks to my apartment.
Easy. This is handled.

Then, they get the couch into my downstairs hallway. And…
"It won't fit," one says in a heavy Romanian accent.
I learn his name is Vlad. I smile awkwardly. Vlad smiles awkwardly.
"Let's try again," the other says. His name is George.

Vlad and George try different angles. Vertical. Horizontal.
Twisting it left and right. Like a rousing game of real life Tetris.
Nothing. They look at me. I'm not the one with the answers.

"What do we do?" I ask.
"You need to call Boris," Vlad says definitively.
"Boris?"
"He can do anything."
"What will he do?"

"He's a carpenter," Vlad explains. "He'll cut the couch into pieces, and put it back together in your apartment."

So, my two options are to leave the very expensive couch on the streets of New York, or to call Boris.

And meanwhile, I just hear this voice in my head… this deep, rich and comforting voice. James Earl Jones, speaking internally to my Soul, saying, *"Keep your center."*

This voice reverberates from my core.
> KEEP.
> YOUR.
> CENTER.

As in, don't freak out. Don't run stories or scenarios through your head. Just stay right here. The center.

I can do that. I call Boris.

I take pictures of the couch and send them to him. He quotes me a fee that stings a little, but I can swing it. Until he realizes, it's a sectional. And he doubles his quote.

Ouch. So much for a free couch.
Maybe life lessons land better when they are more expensive?

Boris tells me he can come over at 12 noon.
Boris shows up around 1 p.m.
With him is his 80-year-old father who's on vacation from Romania and doesn't speak a lick of English.

They start cutting up the big, beautiful, expensive couch in my downstairs hallway. I can't look. What is happening? And maybe it's because I feel ripped to pieces, that watching anything else be cut down and torn apart is hitting a little too close to home.

I hear that voice again. James Earl Jones whispers from the innermost part of who I am, and I hear: *"Trust that a process is unfolding."*

Those words swirl inside of me like a scrolling news ticker. *"There is something bigger going on. Just because you can't see the whole story doesn't mean you're at the ending."*

I feel something inside of me release.

I remember the poet Hafiz said, "This place where you are right now God circled on a map for you."

All day long Boris and his dad from Romania rip up the couch. I decide to leave the apartment because the metaphor is too painful. And even if God circled it, it doesn't mean I have to watch.

When I come back around 5 p.m., one section is done, and the other still needs to be taken apart and reassembled.

Sometimes recovery and restoration takes longer than you thought. And so, I go on with my life while the work is being done. While everything gets torn up and rearranged… I put one foot in front of the other. When I want to start to worry and ruminate or stress and cuss or future-ize, I hear: *"What's the next action?"*

The cool voice of my Soul has something new to whisper to me. It's telling me don't over-analyze, don't dramatize, don't panic. Just do what's next *to be done.*

An inner course correction, keeping me on track.

So, I write emails, run errands, do dishes.

Soon it's 8 p.m. I make dinner while Boris reassembles. He tells me about his girlfriend, their child on the way, leaving his country and starting a new life. He also flirts with me a ton, which is weird and also kind of charming. I feel glad that his 80-year-old father is there with us.

It's fine. It's just a little weird. And honestly, I do feel safe. It just feels like the Divine wanted me to really understand something deeply. And would keep me amused throughout the entire process.

At 9:30 p.m., the couch is back together.
Big and perfect and beautiful in my apartment.
And strangely, there is one cushion missing —
like, even when you think the work is done, there is still more to do.

"It must be in the moving van," Boris tells me.
"Vlad can bring it tomorrow."
And then he asks me out on a date.

I say "thank you," and "no thank you," and "goodnight," and tip him well.

>KEEP YOUR CENTER.
>TRUST THAT A PROCESS IS UNFOLDING.
>WHAT'S THE NEXT ACTION?

I write these on Post-Its and put them up in my apartment.
Little reminders that there is something bigger than me at work.
I have given up needing to know the entire answer. *How do I get from here to there?* My job is to not lose my shit when everything feels like a mess.

Life wants to tear things apart to put them back together. I just gotta listen, connect with the deep peace within me, breathe and trust, and do the next thing, the next action.

Wherever I am led. However long that takes.

It takes a month for me to get the cushion back from Boris to complete the couch. It's not on my timetable. But in that time, Vlad texts about taking me to coffee and George calls and asks if I'd like to go to a museum or a movie sometime. Three date offers from Romanian movers. I don't understand the metaphor in that, but I do think it's funny. Maybe there's not a metaphor. Maybe I'm just cute.

In that same poem, Hafiz goes on to say:
"Our Beloved has bowed there, knowing You were coming."

I think of the Divine Source of love bowing right here, at the large art installment in my living room. A little bit of live theatre, cosmically designed, to remind me that I am being cared for.

It is all a gift for me.
Every bit.
Even the mess.
Especially the mess.

I, like my couch, am being torn apart to be taken somewhere. Somewhere I couldn't get to before. And I can feel the eternal hand of heaven working within to put me back together in a new way.

And that's why I bow every morning to my mother fucking couch.

DATING

I'm just God becoming more aware of God.

And you are just me in another body.
And you are just God becoming more aware of yourself.

And I agree to become more aware of God in you.
Just as I become more aware of God in me.
And you agree to become more aware of God in me.
Just as you become more aware of God in you.

And we both agreed, before we got here,
that I created you, as you created me,
as God created both of us as reflections of Itself.

You desired me before you got here, every part of me — including my
fears, so that through me your Soul could expand, which is really just you
expanding your own Soul, which is really just God expanding into Itself.

And I desired you before I got here, every part of you — including your
fears, so that through you my Soul could expand, which is really just me
expanding my own Soul, which is really just God expanding into Itself.

This push and pull — this courting — this hide-and-seek game with our fear
and our divinity. It's all a show, a game, a charade, in which God
gets to look for God and find Itself in moments of revelation.

There is only a pageant going on. And in the very realization of
the pageant — the show — I draw back the curtain and see
God standing center. And there is no fear, only perfection.

And it's the very fear itself that drives us to look for that perfection.
This is the way we hide our divinity, so we can seek it, and when we
find it, we see God. This is all just the discovery process of God.

Look how you look.
Expand how you expand.
God's process is a perfect one.
And we are both just God becoming more aware of God.

We are each other.
There is no separation.

When we harm, it's ourselves.
When we love, it's ourselves.

RISE

It's Thanksgiving. The large parade balloons lie tied up right outside my apartment. They are lifeless now. Potential. But soon they will launch. And inside, all the feelings are tied up too.

Last night, my love, my partner, was in pain.
Deep pain.
Anger.

His words to me:
You're a liar
I can't trust you
You've ruined my Thanksgiving

I woke up at 4:30 this morning to talk to the Divine. Can I be grateful for even this? The profound pain of intimacy.
I write in my journal and sit with my uncomfortable feelings and get quiet and listen for answers.

In my meditation I hear:
I have to give myself all the things I want him to give me —
understanding, forgiveness, compassion, love — this is my
opportunity to give those things to both of us.
Sometimes you have to be broken open to fully surrender,
to find a new way of working.

When the sun finally rises, I walk through the Upper West Side down Columbus. The sky is barely turning purple and pink. The air is cool, crisp, and full of holiday. Our dreams of cheer still hang suspended.

I pass by a bundled-up father and his daughter, sitting on his shoulders. She wonders if there will ever be a celebration? Is all this cold worth it?

This memory comes to me of being her age. And my father told me to go clean my room. Once there, I was very sure that I could get my stuffed animals to clean for me if I asked them the right way. I laid on my bed, closed my eyes, and tried to use my mind to get my animals to move. My father came in and saw me with my eyes closed, lying on my

bed, yelled at me and beat me. I remember being scared, feeling
powerless, and wondering why he couldn't see that I wasn't
disobeying... Just trying things another way. An experiment.

Why couldn't he see I was good?

I wonder if that was when the mystic in me went into hiding?
The part of me that knew she could move things with her mind.
It wasn't safe to try new things or be powerful.
And so, I turned that part of me off.
It's better that others don't get upset.

Trying things.
Experimentation.
Exploring my powers.
All dangerous.

I think of my father.
And my partner.

My greatest teachers. They are doing their best. I realize they
both lashed out at me, like someone did to them.

God is big enough to hold compassion for us all. And is this an
opportunity? The thing that looks like trauma. The generational
wounds that keep getting passed down, one ancestor to the next.
We're all just doing what we were taught, but how do we rise?

Do we — like the tied-up balloons — have the potential to go higher?
Or is life asking for me to go high
no matter what the circumstance.

Can I love myself and raise myself when it feels scary and heavy in
the world? Can I forgive myself for mistakes, when others won't?
Can I take my child-self in my arms and say, "I will give you
warmth when it's cold outside.
I will bundle you up in love.
Take my hand."

My best friend and I like to tell to each other, *"We can't get upset at our partners for doing their jobs."* If my soulmate's job is to bring up pain to illuminate my wounds for healing, then he's just doing his job. So then, what is my job here?

Maybe it's just to ask the question. To keep walking forward as the crowds surround. To allow this moment to be what it is. To look up, to continue to look up, where there is so much to marvel at...

I feel those knots in my gut.
But in my heart
I know I will rise.
I have a promise to the little girl in me to rise.

CRUCIBLE

I am angry.
I am angry at you for being angry with me.

I am mad.
I am mad at you for being mad at me.

And yes, you have every right to feel what you feel. And so do I.
I have every right to feel angry at the fact that you'd rather have
anger instead of me.

I think you'd rather wear your anger like a badge of how much
you've been hurt and wronged than get to have our love, and
that makes my body burn with a rage that feels so righteous.

But hey, I'm learning to accept my anger.
And that means accepting yours too.
You get to have whatever you choose.

And you chose anger over us. Because
maybe it makes you feel safe or superior or
maybe I just really pissed you off. I feel you holding
onto to it like a security blanket of "how she hurt you"
and "what a bitch she is." I imagine you telling the story a
couple beers in. I guess it felt better to label me than hold me.

And in the very imagining of it I'm judging you, aren't I?
I'm making up a story, aren't I?

Baby, I can't get mad at you for making
up a story, when I'm making up a story.
I forget to see you as innocent, my love.

I'm sorry.

I just don't know how to picture you now.
I don't have a story to make up.
Because the truth is, I don't know.

I feel so confused.
And the only truth is...
I love you.
That's all I got.

I see people around me who want to make up stories. I create stories for
a living. We all want a narrative so we can explain the
unexplainable. Maybe it's not for explaining.

Mystery.
Can I hold it all and not explain it?

Is there anything that's greater than getting to know
yourself and another as Love?

And yeah, we hurt each other, didn't
we, baby? I know I fucked up. I really fucked
up. We didn't get it all alright. Sometimes we acted
out of love. And sometimes we acted out of fear. But we
learned a lot, didn't we? And we are better now for it, aren't we?

We let love do its process on us. And it's still doing its process.
We will carry these lessons into our lives. Into our work. Into the world.

And though I still reach out in the middle of the night,
    craving your smell,
        thinking of your skin,
            dreaming of the way
                you would put my hand
                      on your heart as we slept...
"Thank you" is all I'm left with when the grief has passed.

Thank you for being a miracle in my life.
Thank you for opening yourself to love.
Thank you for teaching me how to release you to your path.

I like to imagine you smiling now. That big beautiful grin on your face,
like when someone's told a joke you like or you're playing music and
feeling free, and there's just pure joy and I feel joy. I am happy when I
think of your happiness.

I hope you find bliss in unexpected places.
I hope strangers make you laugh.
I hope you see a lot of sunrises.

And that many nights you find yourself staring out over expansive vistas and as life feels so very big, it also feels very close and safe.

I hope you feel the arms of infinite love wrapping around you, urging you on. And that really pretty girls flirt with you and you feel handsome and excited and confident. I hope you know how wonderful you are.

Thrive, baby.
Thrive, baby.
I know you're gonna thrive, baby.

That's all I got and it's not a story.
It's the truth. And I'm not even a little bit mad.

We regenerate
when we remember
to see wholeness
in each other.

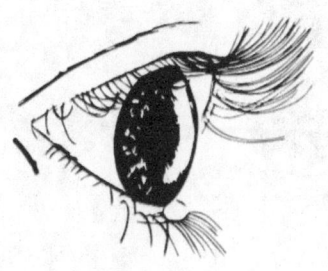
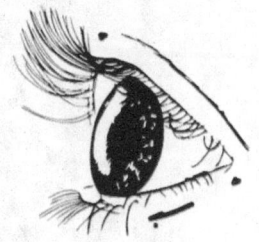

MERCURIAL

My love,
constantly changing
causing me to change.
Doing something to my body that I can't explain.
Causing the deepest part of me to ignite.
Particles immediately rearrange themselves
as if molecules have a memory of ancient chemistry,
of some unseen combustion of heat and wisdom and heavens.

What is it about you? Some hidden magnet that got planted
inside before you came to earth? Activating my animal, my
deepest raw, the private primal roar.

I am transported to the jungle, to the part of me that is still
claw and primate and lion.

You are on the hunt. I want to be your prey.
Sink your teeth into me and draw blood
to the place where our sweat and red and juices mix.

Then suddenly, in a flash, an eyelash blink,
you come closer and I change again.
I become moon dust in your hands.

You bring out of me the ethereal, the part of me that has
no mass, no body. I am the filament of the stars, the light
particles that time and space cannot contain.

You show me who I am before it all began: my original
luminescence. We dance in the nothingness of not here,
my essence intertwined with yours, hovering above the ground.

Half-heaven, half-earth.
All mortal and completely divine.
Born of the flesh, and shot through with eternity.
We are constantly changing, evolving, and being
born again as we rise and fall and rise.

Timeless and temporal
and everything in between,
my love, like mercury.

THE BODY KNOWS

This was worth coming to the planet for: A lover who can drop your
dress in one motion and whispers *"get in the bedroom"* to make
every part of your being get tingly and thrilled.

Does everyone know that sex can be this good? I want to ask other
people when I walk down the street if they feel this feeling too.

"Hello, do you know about the sacredness of multiple orgasms?"

I feel like Maria von Trapp on top of a mountain singing the "The World
is Alive" and now I've realized she was talking about cumming.

I am feeling electricity coming up from the earth as I climb mystical
peaks and stare off into nothing and I know… it's because I have let go.

I have let go of controlling
and being so safe,
of needing to know the ending.
I have let go of giving a shit about form,
and what happens next.

I feel like I'm running through a valley of love-making and I'm romping
with the whole wild world. It's a moving multiple ecstasy that continually
expands upon itself, and —

Fuck convention.
I'm ready for a new path.
There's a trail being blazed from the bohemian inside of me
and I don't know where it goes. But hot damn, my friends, it feels
so good to not know.

This unknown
is teaching me how to listen to a place inside of me,
to delight her,
to please her,
to enjoy her,
to let her live in excitement.

When I look in his eyes and say, *"How do you know how to make
me feel this way,"* and he says, *"Because I'm listening to your body,"*
I just want to tear my hair out and scream!

I can hear my body now too.

It's like someone is fucking the artist
inside of me to new levels of awakening.
It feels like freedom.

I love my life
and I have no idea where it goes.
But I love being on the ride…
I love being in this body.

FOUR INCANTATIONS FOR MY SACRAL CHAKRA

i.

I want to say something out loud and I'm a little scared to say it:
I'm getting really good at sex.

Did I just whisper that? Let me say it louder.
I'M GETTING REALLY GOOD AT SEX.

We weren't taught, as women, that sex was for us, were we?
I don't know about you. Maybe you had really awesome and
progressive parents and they taught you that sex was rad and fun
and holy and beautiful. But it took me a while to figure that out.

I don't know when and where, but
something happened with sex. And with life.

This surrender.
This allowing.
This opening.

And I think it's giving me magical powers.

ii.

And I don't just say that because this thing is happening where I'm having
sex and I can I tune in to see people's past lives, their childhood scars,
their secret dreams, where they are blocked in their energetic anatomy.
You know, that kind of thing... totally normal Tuesday.

I say that because my orgasms have gotten so big and so intense
and so out of control it makes me feel like *I'm magic.*
It makes me feel like I don't even know how immense I am.
It's like there's something in me that is trying to teach me
and it's trying to teach me through sex.

It scares me.

Because aren't we all taught that good girls don't.
And we're supposed to be "pure?"
And we're supposed to save ourselves for something.

But friends, I feel like *I'm saving myself through sex.*

It's bringing me closer to God.
I'm letting my sexuality teach me about where my healing power is,
and how big my creativity is, and what joy is meant to feel like.

And I want to go around and speak to women in hushed tones: "*Hey, come here…
don't listen to what they tell you about sex. It's just not true.*" And the deeper
I go in my meditations, the more free I feel. And the more free I feel, I
don't want, need, or care to listen to anyone else's rules. And the
more open I become to my heart and my pleasure, the more
empowered I feel to create. The more empowered I am.

Sex is teaching me who I am.

iii.

There is a primal teacher in me. She teaches me how to un-do.
How to un-learn. She teaches me about freedom. And bliss.
This primal teacher in me keeps insisting,
"I know what I'm doing. Trust me."

And the same way it is hard to stare at a blank piece of paper,
it is hard to embrace the unknown.
All that creativity.
All those options.
All the possibility.
The uncharted has come to be our teacher.
The empty space has something to give to us.

We feel ourselves want to obtain, achieve.
We want to wrap our arms around a career, money, a person,
because we want so badly to feel that we matter.

The primal teacher in me un-does my arms.
She says, *"I dare you not to hold on."*
She says, *"I crave your space*
and I crave your openness."
She starts laughing.
"My girl, stop working so hard.
Just be still.
Be so still.
You don't need to act like you can't hear.
You came with deep listening.
Listen with everything that you are.
Listen with your whole body.
Surrender to your listening."

The primal teacher is teaching me about my instincts.
She is teaching me about love for my body.
She is teaching me about passion and fearlessness.

The primal teacher is showing me that my power moves through me.
It's there — like lightning — to be conducted by me.
She teaches me about enjoyment, about tasting the moment.
She teaches me that it's all erotic —
being here, being present, writing words, the very
act of creation is alive and happening in all I do.
She never stops doing her job.

The primal teacher in me is teaching me the power of
vulnerability, of freeing the places in me that feel dark.
She's teaching me about non-duality and non-judgement.

She's teaching me how to live.

iv.

It's a hot night and the air feels thick
I'm wearing your t-shirt
Just your t-shirt
Because you told me you had a fantasy of that
And I leave the front door open so a breeze will blow through

And I know that any moment you'll be here
"Hey Babe"
I stand and walk to you as you come through the doorway
Your eyes are so sexy tonight
They are big and open and full
And we are kissing kissing kissing
As your hands reach up under the t-shirt pulling me into you
The front door is still open
As you touch me and I gasp
I reach past you and slam that front door shut
You spin me around and push me up against it
Your fingers inside of m e as our mouths dance
Your breath tastes like mint
Mine like chocolate
And breathing gets heavy and quick
And I feel the ground below my toes get wet
As I rain over your fingers
Then I'm on my knees
And you're in my mouth
And I'm doing what I love most
It's how my lips feel against you
And suddenly we are on the couch
And I'm grabbing over the ledge
And making sounds I don't understand
I'm pretty sure the windows are open
And any neighbors nearby know exactly what's going on
As my nails dig into upholstery
And you tell me how good my ass looks
And we run upstairs
Losing clothes as we go
Because there is air conditioning up there
And you get inside me
And I cum like a dam inside of me has broken open
It feels so good to be broken open…

Afterwards, we lay, all curled up in each other. I like the sound of your voice. I like how our bodies feel. And how it's just easy to be. We talk about our dreams, and how fun it is to be alive.

Downstairs, we sit and I pull cards and read fortunes.
We talk about our secrets, where life is guiding us,
and how the mysteries of it all keep unfolding.
We talk about our childhoods, things we feel shameful about,
our other lovers, and the places where we are growing.

"I have something to tell you," you say.
"Something I've been holding onto for a long time.
You hurt my feelings, like five years ago.
And I pulled away from you and I never told you.
Inside my head, I had the conversation with you like seven times.
But I never told you. And I don't want us to have anything between us."

"What?" I say. "I didn't know.
I can't believe you've been holding onto it.
I love you and I would never want to hurt your feelings.
You mean the world to me. I'm sorry."

He takes my hand. "Have I ever hurt your feelings?"

"Oh yeah," I say, almost laughing.

"When?"

"Yesterday."

"Really?!?"

"Your text. It felt like you were calling me a name. Or that's
what I made up. It felt like you were insulting me."

"I was just protecting myself. I know I can come across
as harsh, but I was teasing you — but really because I
was trying to protect myself."

"Thanks for telling me."

"I love you."

"I love you too."

I can feel our hearts — and our collective heart — opening.
I can feel something so much bigger than us opening.
I melt into the moment. And I allow the moment to melt into me.

In accepting our sexuality,
we also have to accept
ourselves.

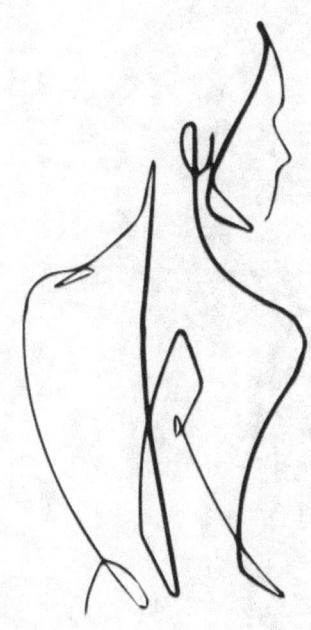

AFFAIRE D'HONNEUR, OR THE HOOK UP

I'm walking under an almost full moon and I hear
the couple behind me stumbling on the grass. She says
"I don't even know where my room is." And I hear him
say, "I've only stayed here once before."

A smile breaks out across my lips. They just met tonight.
I can feel it — too many drinks
and music
and an almost full moon
and they are wobbling towards that thing we all want most
connection
even if its momentary
fleeting
the ability to be affected by another.

There is a sweetness, a preciousness
in all this humanity
in all this fumbling
that makes me want to take everyone up in my arms.

We would all love to do better, wouldn't we?

She'll never know his harsh abandonment. How his father betrayed him.
He'll never know how she became the mother and set the table for
her siblings. But inside this deep longing will be:

See me
the way I wasn't seen
Can you see me?

Maybe you can't.

Maybe we can never fully see each other.
We can try.
We can get quick glimpses.
And still, we will let each other down.

I was supposed to meet someone — a lover — this weekend at this fancy
coastal resort hotel for a getaway and his flight got canceled. When he
called from the airport — so upset — to tell me, I felt a
happiness break open from the center of my heart.

I get to romance myself.

This is what I truly want.
Time to see myself.

Tonight, I walked down to the beach and sat under the slightly-obscured stars.
I saw the smog-filled California night air make the pier lights look blurry
and dream-like. I wandered with no direction, except a gentle nudging
forward from a place inside.

Keep looking, keep going.

I took myself to an outdoor dinner and sat by the fire. I bonded with the
blond sommelier from Australia. We laughed and told stories about
our lives and she said, "I feel like you are already my friend."

After, I laid back in a bubble bath and watched a silly movie.
Then I took a late-night walk, where I discovered my couple
and I wondered about them.

Could they keep going?

What if tonight creates an opening?
And love
true love is planted
and maybe they witness the good
    the wounds
the beauty
    the obsessions
the light
    the fears
in each other.

And they try to let something grow.
Anything is possible.

Maybe that's why we stumble.
We reach.
We get naked.
And we hide.

And we'll do it again.

HALF THE BATTLE

I'm showing up
for myself
and for that which wishes to move through me.

I'm showing up
for the joy
of showing up.

I'm showing up
for love,
to be the presence of love,
to be in love with the presence of love,
to be known by love,
and to express more love.

I'm showing up
to learn.

I'm showing up
for all that I don't know.

I'm showing up
to give something away.

I'm showing up
because I have a vision
and even when I'm afraid,
it never disappears.

I'm showing up
for something to appear
that will bring me to my knees,
leave me in awe,
because I don't know the plan.

I'm showing up
because I am.

I'm showing up
because that's why I came here in the first place.
It's why I decided
to show up.

ATHAME

ATHAME

THE IMPORTANT THINGS

Ooh! I think, *"I have time to write a poem!"* And then the thought
makes me laugh… Like it's a luxury to express myself. Like it's
a luxury to commune with my Soul.

When did I start to think that romancing myself was only for after
all the "work" was done? When the "important" stuff is done?
Because it's never done.

What if this, my poetry, is the most vital thing I do? Because
it keeps me alive. Not alive, like breathing
and heart pumping…

But yes, maybe *truly* breathing. Taking time to breathe. The real breath.
The holy breath. The divine breath of my Spirit.
Yeah, that one…

Not heart pumping like I have a pulse. But heart pumping like
this is what moves me and this is how I stay connected
to what moves me.

What I have realized is that *this* is the most important thing:
That I stay intimately connected and at one with the subtle shifts
within as they whisper secrets to me.

What else is there but distraction?

I came here, to this planet, to be like none other: raging and loud and
unafraid. I came to be triumphantly my very self. Is there a better way
to spend my time than getting to know me today?

So, I sit here and I write a poem.
And I know more about myself than when I started.
And I think this was definitely the very best use of my time.

ME AND TENNESSEE

Want to know a secret?
I see dead people.

Well, that's not exactly true.
But I definitely hear them.
They whisper in my ear.
Now, before you get all weirded out
and call the men in the little white coats to come carry me away,
maybe I should explain…

I believe in things unseen. Like the fact that spirits guard us
and creative muses talk to us in our sleep. I know the world isn't
what it seems in form, and that our path is guarded by forces too
unbelievable to know. I think it's true that souls who have passed
over to the other side enjoy swooping down and hanging out just
for kicks. They come to our parties, and laugh at our jokes — only
the funny ones — but most often, they come down to remind us of
what they spent a lifetime learning.

That's why… Tennessee Williams comes and sits on
my shoulder, every once in a while.

Spirit doesn't weigh anything, so don't worry, I don't get neck
cramps. But sometimes he likes to talk to me. I don't mean this in
any kind of 'he really likes me" sort of way because I know he would
come sit on your shoulder too if you invited him. See, he's a party
boy and he *loves* an invitation. But Tennessee found me when I
was just a lonely little girl and something in him understood me
wanting a friend. He liked my dreaming ways. My all-too-romantic,
read-me-a-poem, lost-in-a-fantasy-world ways. And so Tennessee,
decided he'd come and frequent. He hangs out on my right shoulder
from time to time. I can feel him. And he talks to me about loneliness
and cute boys and magic and the unrelenting desire to be understood.

I hadn't heard from him in quite a while.
Then, the other day, just to pass the time,
my friend put a thick book in my hand.
Tennessee William's published notebooks.
Oh, he kept a journal for his entire life?
Me too, I think, as I look to my right.
Me and you, Tennessee. You and me.

So I crack open the book...

And then *oh!*
I can feel you, my friend,
as I thumb through the pages.
The self-doubt.
Your pages are so full of...
    I don't know if I can
You didn't trust yourself, did you?
    Shouldn't even write
And fear would creep up on the inside
    What's the point?
You had days you couldn't do anything
    I should give it up
but cry in a ball on your bed,
    Criticized again
shaken by anxiety,
    Not good enough, not good enough, not good enough
obliterated with despair.

Oh Tennessee, you are my reminder that it is never about our doubt.
It is about our ability to go on. And any fear of failure can never conquer
us unless we decide it can. When we give up, that's when greatness loses.

Tennessee knows. And he's sitting on my shoulder telling me he would've
drank a lot less if he knew that everybody felt that way sometimes.
See, he believes, like me, that greatness runs deep in all of us.
We all have the ability to be the next legend and we hear the call
inside of us dying to come out.

Because, just like Tennessee, even when you can't see greatness,
it's there. And if you look really closely to the person next to you,
you can see their greatness burning in their eyes,
Go ahead and look. I'm serious.

LOOK.

To the person next to you.
See what's going on underneath?
Can you see their greatness?
I bet you can if you look long enough.
Can you hear their quiet hopes and dreams?
Keep looking.
Can you feel the legend that wants to be set free?

And as my Tennessee said, *"Weak beautiful people, who give up with such grace. What you need is someone to take hold of you — gently, with love, and hand your life back to you."*

I say we take life by the throat and hold on tight. I say we make a commitment to each other not to give up on ourselves. I say we open our mouths so wide to be heard and open our hearts so far to be love that we rip through the doubt, break open the dam of our fears, until our light shines with so much force that we transform the world with who we are.

We are not those who hide our greatness.
We let our light shine.

And, as another great book says, *"If you bring forth what is within you, what is within you will save you. If you do not bring forth what is within you, what is within you will destroy you."*

And I know that's what happened to my friend Tennessee.

Alcohol and pills didn't destroy him. He was destroyed because after all the fame he became paralyzed by fear. He couldn't let what was in him come out anymore, and it killed him. And that's why he follows me around like Jacob Marley, sometimes clanking chains because he thinks it's funny. He wants to get my attention, so I'll get your attention and tell you:

Stop suffering, he did it already.
Stop doubting yourself, it's just a waste of time.
And don't be tortured, or if you have to, just have a
really good sense of humor about it.
And start creating now.
Bring forth what is in you right now.
With abandonment.
And joy.
And freedom.
Because, as Tennessee said, *"to be free is to have achieved your life."*

And so, I'll add, "Then what are we waiting for?"

We all are so much. And if we are not accepting our greatness,
then we are suppressing our greatness with our doubt.
And it's time to let go and be set free to our greatest yet to be.

If one of our supreme dramatists was afraid he couldn't write, what
do you have bubbling inside of you that you are afraid you can't do?
And just how many are the next great gifts that life wants to give?
Go ahead and raise your hands. You know you want to.

Yeah, that makes him smile.
He told me.

And that's why I talk to dead people.
Sometimes it's the dead that remind me to live.

Oh, what's that?

Sorry. One last word from Tennessee.

He says, *"Success is shy — it won't come out while you're watching."*

And so, he advises, that we should quit watching for it, quit looking for it,
and just be so much ourselves — shining so brightly —
that success wanders over, comes and finds us, and we're like,
"Oh, I was so busy being myself, I almost didn't notice you."

DOWNLOAD THIS

Oh Great Goddess! Please write me! I would like a daily email,
like hmmm... Instructions from the Goddess Ship.

In this email, you would tell me exactly what to do, where to go, and that's
what I would do! I would be so faithful to these daily instructions
if you could just be so clear.

Free will is a bitch sometimes.

I didn't get answers in my inbox today, but I did get a little wink from my
Divine Mama. I had lunch with a multi-millionaire. Successful dude.
You know how that goes. I asked him about his life
and I asked him about his business.

"Do you ever feel like you are doing too much?"

"All the time," he said, in confidence. "Every day my list of things
to do never gets done."

I felt... something inside of me relax.

Sometimes I'm a little tough on myself. I think that my falling in love with
so many things is a problem. "You do too much," I scold myself.
Like somehow, if I could just do less, my life would be better.

That isn't how the Goddess thinks. My Earth Mother Mama is a massive
multi-tasker. She creates all over everywhere, and she doesn't
think twice about it. She is spontaneously creating
out of love at all times... and so am I.

I, and my Mother, are one.

And as I heard this millionaire dude talk, I suddenly felt like I didn't have
a fatal flaw. There isn't any problem in my wanting to do all the things.
Maybe I just need to stop scolding myself and start celebrating myself
instead. Maybe it's time to give myself permission to be myself.

Can you imagine if we scolded Mother Earth for creating everywhere?
Can you imagine if we told her to stop being in love
with the entire Universe?

Now, I know I don't really need a daily email. I have inner instructions
and it's called desire. A force of unquenchable yearning that guides me
and directs my actions. Always energizing me. Always prompting
me where to go, what to do, and what choices to make.

This is the Inner Goddess. The Inner Mother. She is righteous and right
acting. And holy. And like any good goddess, from Aphrodite to
Lakshmi, she loves to be lauded and affirmed.

Maybe it's time to turn the question around…
Oh sweet desire, what is your request?

May I be faithful to that part in me.
May I learn how to listen to the memorandum from within.

Right here and now
is the best party ever created.

And all I have to do
is invite myself in.

MAGIC LESSONS

This city is bewitched.
But guess what? So is every city.
Even the places so small, they aren't even cities.
Like the ground you are standing on right now.

Look down.
Under your feet.
Yeah, there's dirt, dust, gum wrappers, dead leaves.
And you know what else?

There's magic there.

I know this because, earlier this year,
I told the Universe I wanted to understand
the finer points of sorcery.

I wanted to know the deepest secrets,
say the incantations,
hold wonder in my hands,
and let starlight radiate off my fingertips.

I wanted to be a true alchemist of creation
like a mother fucking buddha who could levitate!
And as I asked, like a cosmic proclamation to the skies
(or to my journal, to be more exact!),
it answered in a big lesson in…

Detachment.

Let me tell you, detachment is a whole lot less sexy than magic.
At least, that's what I thought.

Until this arrived one fall morning…

"When we get into clinging, we get out of connection."

I wrote that phrase down in the notes section of my iPhone
one early Monday on the C train
as a reminder of my lessons in conjuring.

This year, all the hard-won studies came in the form of

Let go. Let go. Let go.
It was the reoccurring click-clack of the subway tracks:

detach detach detach.

As if the entire city is the voice of the Universe reminding me,
"When you are holding on in your mind to *over there*, you can't be *here*...
And *here* is where the *magic* is.
Here is where you want to be."

I got to learn the tough way that when I think my good has to come from
a particular person, place, or thing, I'm screwed.
Because right now, *this* moment of connection, is where my power is.

So whether it's how my career unfolds,
if the movie is finally greenlit,
or if my lover ever texts me back —
I'm learning to live life with an open hand.

Connection with something deeper, fully alive, and happening now,
that's the heartbeat of this beautiful planet.
And it's happening everywhere.
Not just for me.
It's for all of us.

Connection with ourselves,
with strangers on the C train,
with the great unknown
all around and through us.

Everything else is illusion.

Everything else gets in the way of magic.

PYROTECHNICS

Remember when you were a kid
and you would try to describe the fireworks?

Hey, that looks like an imploding star of purple ice!
    Oh, and that one looks like a dancing lion's head!
        And... and...
            And this one is...
                A burning yellow palm tree!

A momentary trace of the rocket. The huge burst of stars. Cascades of screams and awe. It all fades. It all passes.

"This too shall pass," my grandma used to tell me as a kid. I think it's in the Bible somewhere. I hear the echo of her scratchy voice as I look up.

Yep, these pyrotechnics are only moving through.
Everything that's exploding in our lives, one day won't be.

We are not the fireworks. We are the sky.
And the events we want to call out as

Challenges
    Wounds
        Endings

are just part of this Epic Light Show. Fireworks flashing.
And then *Poof*... One day, gone.

Even the residue of grey smoke blows away.
Only the memory remains.

If the thing that stays with me is the recollection of what I saw, doesn't that mean I get to choose? My perception is mine.

I get to name those flashes. So, when bombs go off in my life like it's the 4th of July, I got a new game I wanna play:

Rename the Rockets

So, if it's failure that flares,
    I choose to call it Priceless Wisdom.
If something lights up like loss,
    I dub it Making Space for Something Better
If it bursts big like betrayal,
    a Lesson in Forgiveness and Setting Free
and if this evening's display is death,
    let's try Rebirth and Transformation.

Because the names I give the things that happen in my life, determine
the spectacle. That's right, my eyes are the most powerful tool
of creation I have and my vision reforms phenomena.

So as the dancing colors pass, I can enjoy my front seat to this
once-in-a-lifetime show. These rockets are beautiful, my friends.
Even when the noise is scary. It's all going to vanish anyway.

And when I look up...

Suddenly I'm seven
    walking back to the parking lot holding Grandma's hand
        She points out
            Silver Spiders
            Blue Rain

Grandma is now 101 years old. She lies in bed, her eyesight gone, still
drinking her red wine. Her mind sparks and disappears so quickly.
That body is evaporating before me.

And I wonder when she closes her eyes and looks back on her
life, if all she can see is the beauty?

love is here.
love is here.
love is always

right here.

SEEK FIRST

I remember this moment in my life where it felt like I had nothing.
Like I was doing life totally wrong —
sleeping on my best friend's couch
and feeling like a Big Fat F.

And this Bible verse from back when I was a little kid in
Sunday School came echoing into my head:

Seek first the kingdom of God and his righteousness,
and all these things will be added unto you.

Well, that seemed like an easy equation.
Seek God.
Do right things.
Get the stuff.

Nothing else I was doing was working,
so, I thought I'd try that for a while.

I started reading.
And listening.
And studying.

And they told me to forgive,
so, I thought I'd try that.

And then I found I was being led.
And then I found I was transforming.

My life was becoming something new.
There was a Me being released from the center of my Soul.
And she was who I *really* was.

And my unhealed places started coming up to be healed.
And yeah, that sucked.
I spent some time on the bathroom floor in tears.
And I went to some 12 Step meetings.
More forgiving.

And otherworldly voices started speaking to me.
I started listening.
And they told me to teach.
And I didn't want to.

I kept learning.
And I started teaching.

And my biggest dreams started coming true and leaving me in awe.
And I fell in love.
And I made a shit ton of money.

And then *more* unhealed places came up to be healed.
And it got even more painful.
And I went to more 12 Step meetings.
And therapy.
And forgave again.

And fell out of love.
And lost money.

And my dreams started to change and evolve.

And I kept reading.
And studying.
But playing more.
And resting more.
And receiving more.
And honoring more.
And being more.

I laid on the grass and stared at the clouds and felt ridiculously happy.

I was undoing more.

And then I started questioning all of my conditioning.
And questioning my preferences.

I became more rebellious.
I became more unconventional.
And undid all my rules.
And followed my charms.
And became more and more child-like.

And when others asked, I told them they could
do the same if it looked like fun to them.

And people followed.
And I fell in love again.
I fell in love with everyone.
And I started letting creativity be fun for its own sake.

I watched miracles happen every day and knew that they would.

And more fucking unhealed places kept coming up to be healed.
And are we doing this *again?!*

And became more okay with my anger.
And my emotions.
And observed them with more compassion.

Learning to love those scared places in me.
Learning to love the part of me that wants to get it right.
More 12 Step meetings.

Can I live in a state of forgiveness?

And stopped taking it all so seriously.
And started having fun with the light show as it passed before my eyes.
It all became more of a comedy.

I'm learning to allow life to have its way with me.

And the kingdom that I'm seeking now is not some faraway place.
And the definition of God is goodness that is always present.
And so, the kingdom of God that I'm seeking is the
good that is always here and now.

And righteousness has become "right seeing."
So, may I have the right seeing to be aware that good is always here and now.

And trust that everything I might ever need will find me.

And know that I have it all already.

Oh, I get it.

I already have it, so there's nothing to seek.

A NEW FRIEND

I met someone today.
Well, someone kicked my door down and met me.
It was my Powerful Self.
She's not the kinda bitch you mess with.

I asked if she'd be my new friend, and she snarled,
>   *That's a stupid question.*

And then, she winked at me, to let me know she's always been my friend.

But she was pretty pissed
because I kept her locked down,
pushed down,
put down
for so long
under politeness,
and she was about to fucking scream.

>   *No! No more!*

My Powerful Self leaped up and declared,

>   *I'm in charge now!*
>   *No more playing small.*
>   *I was sent here to get shit done!*

I mean, that chick doesn't mess around.
She knows the entire Universe has her back,
and so, she struts with the confidence of a woman on a mission.

Because she is.
And she knows.
She came here for a specific reason.
Like a jacked-up Joan of Arc.

She's talking about revolution.
And she came here to stand for change.

She presses her ear up against the silence
Listening for the still truth that is always being transmitted,
So she can not-so-gently grab a bullhorn
and scream into it with the reverence of Joan Jett:

> *I HAVE A MESSAGE FOR YOU*
> *We need what's in you!*
> *Yes, you!*
> *I'm talking to you!*
> *I know you are afraid, my love.*
> *I am too.*
> *It's okay.*
> *We can be afraid together.*
> *But sister, no more blending in.*
> *There isn't time.*
> *No more staying quiet.*
> *The work is too important.*
> *No more pretending you don't know.*
> *Damn it, you know!*
> *You came in KNOWING!*
> *And someone out there needs to know what you KNOW!*

See, there's this Powerful Self in me and she won't shut up.
She just wants to wear high-heeled stilettos and a short skirt
and she came to call-up, call-out the Powerful Self in you!

Because we all came for rebellion.
We came to yank people out of complacency.
We came to shock people out of their sleep.

Insubordination is the new frontier
and there is an uprising coming from another kind of consciousness.
They say the door to liberation swings inward,
and waiting in the home of your heart
is a Tough Ass Mother who wants to shake the world to its core.

Don't push down the things that make you special.
Don't smooth out those corners,
Be jagged. Be sharp. Be freaky.
Let them be scared of you.
And don't give a fuck!

There's a new friend in town.

And she's not the kinda bitch you mess with.

AND THEN SHE SAID...

"Whenever we reveal who we really are, it expands everyone else."

She tells me this right after our morning walk along the canals and I tell this woman I just met how I've been practicing polyamory. Something inside just told me to share it. Like I'm tired of telling half-truths. And I just wanna tell people who I really am when they ask. And not edit my answers based on what I think they might say.

And when someone asks about my romantic situation and I say, "I have a boyfriend," it's like I chickened out. I shrunk. I'm showing this person a little sliver of who I am when I'm the whole fucking cosmos...

So, imagine my surprise, when I tell her the truth, and she lifts her arms into the sky and screams: "I NEEDED TO HEAR THAT! TELL ME EVERYTHING!"

And on this morning walk, in these canals in Colorado, I'm laughing on the inside... *Who knew?*
When I am transparent, it is a gift.
It's a hard thing to believe. That my truth won't scare or offend or push away.

Where did we learn to hide our truth?
When did we first start getting punished for who we truly are?
When did we learn to prioritize other people's goals and desires for us over our own?

I feel in the quiet places of myself... an evolution. The desire to please others is melting away, and what is growing in its place is a desire to please myself. To ask myself what I want... and to give that to myself.

And I wonder? Is there is a moment — a crucial, defining moment as children — where we put our deepest and dearest selves into hiding because it upsets others? And then, I wonder...is true maturation about rediscovering who we were before we learned to compromise our Soul?

There is a definition of love
that means freedom.

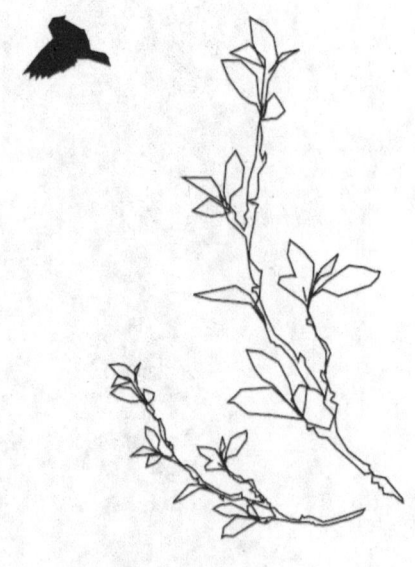

right now
since you've started reading this poem
I have fallen in love with you.

And now, I give myself love
without form
without shape
without definition
without possessiveness

I know that love and freedom are the same thing.

My Soul really wants to be free,
and only I can grant that permission for freedom.
My Soul really wants to love,
and only I can grant that permission to love.

"Whenever we reveal who we really are, it expands everyone else."

Who I am is someone looking to expand myself.

I hear a term on TV: *Individuation*.
I look it up, because on some level, I know it's for me.
Carl Jung talked about it in terms of self-actualization.
It means the process of becoming who we are, separate from others.
When we believe what we believe.
When we know what we came for.
Listening to our inner voice.
Even if others around us disagree.

It's all a grand experiment. I know that.

Lately, I discover that I desire silence and alone time more and more.
I know my biggest addiction is having a schedule that is jammed packed
full with appointments and meetings and obligations… When I just want
to walk out into nature by myself and hear what my Soul
has to say. It's like I'm asking everything else to fade
into the background so I can truly hear.

Undoing the wounds of codependency is no easy task.

And when I'm free and unencumbered,
I find it so easy to slip into deep appreciation of the moment.
The way the sun feels on my shoulders.
The crunching of dry leaves under my feet.
The simple breath — in and out.

I have spent so much of my life in striving. Trying to earn something.
Approval. Love. Deservingness.
The more I give those things to myself,
the less I want or need from the world.

And so, I give it all up.
I'm on strike from striving!
From this moment on, in the canals of Colorado!

Here's the truth:
I fall in love
everywhere
all the time
I just love to love
it makes me happy

GROW OURSELVES BEAUTIFUL

I wish someone could have told me when I first started out, that
I had one primary job on this planet: to Grow Myself Beautiful.

That it would be impossible
    to Grow the World Beautiful,
    or Grow a Family Beautiful,
    or Grow a Project Beautiful
if I first didn't start with me.

Me.
I'm my own garden.

Here's how I learned this lesson at 40:
    I set a boundary.
    I think it might have been my first one.
    I felt very clear when I set it.
    It came up from the still and peaceful place deep
    within that gives zero fucks and said:
    This Is The Truth.
And the moment I said it, I felt free.

See, before all this, I was just so proud of my sweet garden, I wanted to share
it with the world! Come smell the beautiful hydrangea! Enjoy the colors
of the carnations! Everybody dance the dance of the lilies!

But someone got a little careless. I forgave, because I know that my
garden springs eternal. It reanimates and reproduces every day…
but after a while, carelessness takes its toll. It hurts to get stepped on.
I watched my flowers fall over under the stomp of heavy shoes.
Nothing can truly thrive if people keep trampling.

So, I erected a fence. It's beautiful and white and feminine and strong.
It stands tall and proud. It loves to be a protector. And it has a delicate
gate, that swings open, because I love to invite people to come over
and play. It is easily accessible on purpose.

But I get to decide when the gate opens.

I learned that responsibility starts with me. I just never knew before that I needed a fence. I had been staying away from boundaries because I love freedom so much. But here's the secret I learned...

I discovered my new fence helps my garden to grow.

And with a little bit of mindful care, everything flourishes.

Now, I find an oasis: lush and vibrant and exuberant —
    and it keeps germinating
    and sprouting
    and bearing more fruit.
I didn't know it could get this beautiful.

So I invite the entire neighborhood. It's a community garden for people who have a shared respect to come be in joy and frolic and feast.

We all get to reap.
We all get to prosper.
And I'll never be hungry again.

My true vocation is to be a gardener of the Soul.

COAXING

Do we all just spend our whole lives trying to figure out who we are?
To unwrap ourselves and see what's on the inside? I feel like my truest
purpose these days is to know myself. Experience myself.

It's like I've wrapped myself up... *In what?* Fear? Obligation? Duty?
A straight jacket of conditioning? And now — piece by piece — I take
off another layer of hiding.

Tearing off the people pleasing...
Ripping through the expectations...
Peeking in past the addictions...

Who is in there? What do you want?

And as I watch myself get closer to me, I find she's unwrapping herself from
the inside. There is someone within, clawing her way out. Trying to
break through. I can feel the real woman within getting empowered.
And she emerges at the promise of a good time.

And so, I make a vow to fill my life with the things I love,
and be brave enough to let go of things that don't.
I break the bonds of just dealing...
    of just obligation...
    of just getting by...
    of numbing...
    just settling.
No more tightly tucked paper corners.

May my entire existence be filled with the things that make me
say FUCK YEAH! I'm breaking through complacency to find I am
the best present I ever gave myself. Every time I allow joy to
be my motivating factor, I set myself free.

There is no time to waste. Our massive potential is actualized
and energized and liberated by what turns us on.

We came here to be LOVE.
> *Unwrap*

To create from LOVE.
> *Unwrap*

To let what we LOVE lead us.
> *Unwrap*

By acknowledging and following what we love we not only *know* ourselves, we *free* ourselves.

Let me be brave enough to see who is inside.

THE GOLDEN ELIXIR

LOVE IS HERE

Right now on the subway there are faces that
look tired, distracted, worried...
but if I look deeper...

Love.

In that woman texting who picked out that green skirt with the polka dots to wear this morning because she likes it, damn it. I can tell she likes it. It flares on the bottom and I wonder if she twirls in front of the mirror when she puts it on?

Or, in the two best friends, dressed alike: matching black lace stockings, matching red-orange lipstick, matching haircut with blunt bangs that I could never pull off. With a look, not even a nod, they agree this is their stop. They hop off the train in formation, Their movement perfectly synced, and I wonder how many hours it took to get that close?

In the three little girls, sisters, I'm sure, all with big eyes, taking turns to whisper secrets to their father. Manhattan adventures still live on their faces. The middle sister leans back on the subway bench and curls up against her big sister. Her head effortlessly winds into her sister's neck. I see pieces of myself in the littlest one. She wears an over-sized red hat on her head like a drunk Santa Claus, swaying to the tune of her own tipsy drummer. And I wonder if Dad, looking at his three little miracles, feels in awe of what he's created?

Love.

In our surprise conversation last night... Searching, honest, and without answers. He reached across the table and took my hand, or maybe I took his. The look in his eyes as he said, "This is sacred." And I wonder if it's okay that we don't know what we are doing? Or what we are supposed to be? Is there space for the unknown here too?

I ascend the subway stairs and let the wind gently blow me down the sidewalk. I notice the way the sunset paints the top of the buildings pink.

I'm romanced by the smell of roasted cashews from the cart on the corner and I dance to the taxicab horns. The city kisses me so passionately.

Louis Armstrong hums softly in my earbuds.

Love is here. Love is here. Love is always right here.

when we get into clinging,
we get out of connection.

AN AFFAIR TO REMEMBER

Do you know what I love?
Being with myself.

The warmth of my own company, nurturing little ol' me. I'd like a table for one, please. I'll light some candles, play a vintage record, and slip into a hot bath... I can never get enough of my love.

Now, I adore people. I live for conversations with strangers whose stories are all so unique, or an early morning breakfast of cappuccinos and croissants with my best girl. I like late-into-the-night deep talks on the phone with a handsome long-haired man or getting lost & found in a foreign country with other travelers. There's bliss to be had in window shopping the day away, or stumbling upon a bit of wonder. Give me a dance party full of sweaty bodies jumping to the don't-stop-won't-stop-music. Kissing and kissing and kissing untill we don't know whose lips are whose
or where the perimeters of our faces end. I love being amazed
by everything I do not know.

Basically, I dig all good stuff.
But coming home to me is like really coming home.

And nothing can surpass the peace I feel when my Soul gets to sing its own song. Like taking myself for a walk in Central Park. Or a gorgeous cup of tea for one, shoes off, hair down, while my favorite blanket holds me tight. I'm just so nice to come home to.

The sweet nothings I whisper to me are the most delicious.

And I remember myself,
the tenderness of my heart,
the call of my purpose,
when I'm alone.

Where are you gonna take me?
What are we gonna do?

Let me get quiet enough to hear me.
Let me get still enough to feel my love.

A NEW WAY OF SEEING

I can't help but see
                love descending all around me
           like multi-colored flowers
                                      falling from the sky.

I drive through this big bright blue morning
                  which embraces me
          with open arms and I can feel the child inside me
                                screaming

Does it really get this good?

                    Yes, it does, is the message in every face.

        Yes, it does, echoed in every moment.

It's like the world has woken me
                     up to the perfection that is everywhere.

            And I want to tell everyone I meet
                  Do you see?
                  Do you see?
                  Do you see?

                                    All this joy is inside of me.
                    And I'm just a reflection of who you are.

INVITATION

I have an invitation… for myself.
It's called "Fall in love with now."
And it's time to open up the envelope and see what's there.

At first glance, this note may seem crisp and white and even nondescript, but it's a blank slate that has been waiting just for me. So, let's RSVP. I'll put on my fancy shoes, dress head-to-toe in sequins and feathers, and step right in…

Because I know that this gala I'm inviting myself to is only as full as the fun I'm having — the delight I'm dishing out — the bigness of the banquet that I'm bringing — not next year, not next week, but *now*. This second.

The festivities start here.

It's like I get glimpses of opening the doors to this celebration of the century where I see so clearly how much beauty is everywhere, how much love is omnipresent, how much opportunity is all around. And I'm ready to dance the night away.

The music of life's best DJ is pumping in my Soul…
Its rhythm says,

> *It's all up to YOU, girl*
> *You wanna give everything in that dynamic heart of yours?*
> *How present can you be?*
> *How groovy can you get?*
> *How much mess can you make?*
> *At this all night jam, we are FEARLESS, baby girl.*
> *We leave it ALL on the dance floor.*
> *You can be fearless…*
> *Do that back bend.*

Because I know I'm slamming the door shut on this blowout every time I'm judging the moment, when I'm living in the past somewhere, or worried about the future. When I got an agenda on how things should be.

What if every person I meet is the dance partner I've been waiting for?
What if every interaction I have is the hottest rendezvous of the evening?
What if every beat is another mystery seducing me further into the song?

The rhythm says,

> *Go for it.*
> *Be clumsy.*
> *Step on your own feet.*
> *Eyes closed. Eyes open.*
> *Let your judgement come up.*
> *Yeah… watch it.*
> *Dance with it.*
> *Let your silliness come up.*
> *Yeah… Enjoy it.*
> *Relish it.*
> *Go big,*
> *Or go small,*
> *Let your body lead you.*
> *She wants to lead.*
> *Let your sexiness, your craving, and your hunger find expression.*
> *Try it all on,*
> *Shake it all off.*
> *It all wants to move.*
> *How does it want to move?*
> *How does it feel to move?*
> *Where does the movement take you when you let it?*

I am inviting myself to fall in love with the moment.

To open.
To open.
To open.

And enter this shindig completely unprotected and undefended.
To revere completely what is.

Right here and now, is the best party ever created.
And all I have to do is invite myself in…

Stop ~~——~~ doubting ~~——~~
~~——~~ yourself, ~~————~~
~~————————~~
~~——~~ it's ~~——~~ just ~~——~~
a waste ~~——————~~.
~~————————~~
~~——~~ of ~~——~~
~~————~~ time. ~~~~

LOVE HIGH

My love affair with the Divine is like permission to get high off of life.

Forget smoking a tightly-rolled j, or one of those cute vape pens, or even a tasty gummy, the buzz I feel when I fully enter love... *Woo! It is euphoria on steroids!* It's my real and true state. It is who I am. First and foremost. The high-flying energy of pure unconditional love.

I have done enough molly to know it's a good time, but not as good as —

Wait! Can we talk about "unconditional" for a moment? As in, it doesn't matter what's happening. It's not based on circumstances, the outer world, or anything in form. It's not based on how that person treated me, or what my bank account is doing, or what's in the headlines today. There's no condition that I want to allow to get in between me and the love that I am.

See, there's a huge force of glowing, flowing light emanating from my innermost core. It is tremendous aliveness and vitality and it is bliss. And I know, when I am not feeling it, it's because — somehow, someway — I cut myself off from it. I am the only person who can.

See, that juice drips directly from the Source. Always.
And the only thing I ever need to do is give myself access to it.
It's right there.

And I didn't even meditate today. I talked and listened about prayer, and exercised, and laughed in the sun with my girlfriends.
And all of that is free. I just opened up my heart, and
I didn't give myself any excuse to close it.

And then, *wham!*

The rush of love is life's free offering.
Available at all times.

Love allows.
Love grants.
Love gives.
Love frees.
Love *moves*.

May I be wise enough to remember that it is never about conditions.
May I be wise enough to give myself permission to be in love.
May I be wise enough to go within where the best high lives.

REGENERATION

I like to get up early. I like the cold creaking floorboards under my feet.
The smell of freshly ground coffee beans. That sip from the first cup as the
steam rises up. The glow of the sunlight peeking through the curtains.
It says, "Good Morning, Kristin."

I hear it. Cause there I am.

Nothing is better than that feeling of finding yourself. I always sneak up
on myself so unexpectedly. Like when I open up the door in the morning,
look up into the trees and breath in that crisp brand-spanking-new air.

Oh, there I am!

Walking out into the world in my cutest outfit, sure of my fullness and that
I'm shining from within. There I am! Telling the truth to someone
when I know they need to hear it. There I am. Hearing the truth
from someone when I really need to hear it.

Yeah, there I am.

I remember
I remember
I remember

It's like regeneration, isn't it?
That starfish who loses its point and it grows back, all by itself.

Regeneration.

Do we, like the starfish, break off a piece of ourselves
when we forget our wholeness? When we forget our
massiveness? When we forget our connectedness?
When we think for a moment that we're limited, we're
like that star that lost its point... and we drift through
life, four points, not five, wondering why it's such a
struggle to get anywhere. Why am I floundering?
Shouldn't it be easier than all this? Lost in the ocean,
feeling pointless, and we don't remember who we are.

And then, in a split second, a divine moment happens,
and suddenly... *we remember.*

There I am.
Regeneration. A fully formed star. My God, we always have
the possibility of rediscovering ourselves at any moment.

We are always only this far away from wholeness.
We are always only this far away from whatever it is we feel we lack.
We are always only this far away from being a fully formed star.

Let's remember ourselves.

I remember you.
There you are.
I see you fully formed.
Perfect.
Complete.
A star.

And I will hold this vision of you so when you forget, I can remind you:
you're perfect. And that will help me remember, so I can look in the mirror
and see myself totally completely one hundred percent perfect.

There I am.

And I ask that you hold this vision of me so when I forget — and
boy, do I forget — you can remind me too. It can be a promise
we make together to see ourselves as perfect.
To see ourselves as complete.
To see ourselves as stars.

We regenerate when we remember to see wholeness in each other.

Oh, there I am.
Oh, there you are.
Oh, there we are again.

Maybe that's why it's important we forget, so we can have the opportunity
to remind each other. We get to remember our divinity by being God
for each other. We all remember we're stars together.

And I wonder, in all this forgetting and remembering: is it God, always leading us back to ourselves or is it us… are we always leading ourselves back to God?

I don't know, maybe you can help me remember.

Maybe the storm
has its own joy.

STORY TELLERS

"We project our darkness onto others and then we banish them for it."

The writer tells me this at lunch at the Chateau Marmont and I almost choke on my salad. I write it down on my yellow legal pad because it hits so close to home.

The wisdom of the Universe takes me to fancy LA landmarks where the sunlight hits the lunch table like a Hollywood spotlight. I can almost hear the unseen director:

"Pay attention. This is about you."

                                                                 PULL BACK BIRD'S EYE POV:

I wonder... where did this idea come from? That we need to protect ourselves?
    Where did defensive living come from?

It's like I'm walking on a set filled with hazy fog... like something out of Casablanca. And I wonder, have I been saying someone else's lines for a long time?

Somewhere early on, I learned that if someone doesn't do what you like, or want, or if you feel hurt, you pull away. You punish when you don't approve. When things don't meet your preference or survive your judgement.

Oh my god. Deep underneath all this talk of love, I was taught and conditioned to condemn.

                                                                         AND ZOOM IN:

Do I do that to myself? Do I withdraw love or connection from myself when I feel like I'm being "bad" or undeserving? Am I afraid of being hurt by you? Am I afraid of being hurt by me? Are we just wearing the roles assigned to ourselves as victim and perpetrator, and we cast the other as the opposite?

We create dramas and wars, scripting narratives because it's easier
to point the finger than discover the darkness within us.

CLOSE ON:

The darkness in me.
And shit, yeah, there *is* darkness in me.

It's crafty.
It hides.
It dresses itself up as "self-righteousness" and "knowing."

Oh, sweet darkness, get in my arms, and let me love you.
Just let me love you.
You are mine.

It's time to stop playing make-believe, Kristin.
Everything I see in another is me.

DISSOLVE TO:

The wise ol' Universe takes me further into Hollywood that
evening, where a very sexy man says to a large group of people:

*"The heart can't be hurt and the soul can't be tarnished.
Our true self is like a diamond in a world of pillows."*

What if… I've been living in an illusion of "otherness"?
What if… "You" are just a part of me that needs love?
What if… Every time I want to judge and pull away, it's actually
time to embrace and pull close?

As Ram Dass said, we're all just *"God in drag."*

Here in Hollywood there are a lot of costumes. A lot of ways
to contort the plot. But underneath it all, there is a
new story that wants to be told.

Inclusion. Oneness. Interconnectedness. Expansion.

I am ready to put down the script.
The old storyline isn't mine.

THAT FLOWER NEXT

I had this dream.

I'm not sure if I was even fully awake or asleep but I was lying in bed... and I had this vision. It was a glowing ball of energy. That energy was made up of string, so tiny, like hair, like radiant filaments. This electric string was wrapped around itself, again and again, creating billions or trillions of concentric circles, all attached. All one.

The ball was vibrating. Alive.

And then, like zooming in on a microscopic piece of this pulsating string... a tiny fraction of one represented a human life.

Where a Soul came through a body...
    dropping through,
        passing through,
            cycling through
                from one incarnation to another...
as if the string was made up of all our lives.

And the Soul just went...
    like going through a hollow tube,
        from one life,
           to another life,
                to another life...
and the energy moved so fast.

So fast!

The ball represented every incarnation from the beginning of human life to the end of human life. And it was all happening at the same time.

And this energy that we all are... got to pass through every incarnation.

As in, my Soul, gets to be every person that's ever been
   from the beginning of time, to the end of time,
      as does your Soul.
         As does his.
            And hers.

And what is gender anymore?

We just keep going around and around and around until we've all done the entire cycle. And that's why you can't run out of time.

In my dream, we all get the chance to be each other.

And we've all gotten to do the kindest and most selfless and brave and wise acts ever done. We all got to be Martin Luther King, Jr. and Muhammad and Helen Keller and Bhagat Singh and Marie Curie.

And we've also all done the most horrific and insane things and unspeakable things. We've all been Joseph Stalin and Fidel Castro and Mary Ann Cotton and Charles Manson.

We've all done it all, from the beginning of time to the end, until we all know every facet of the human experience. And we keep cycling through.

And in this dream, or vision, we were all trying to teach each other.
Leave clues for each other of what we've learned. So that each time we pass through, we could do it a little better.
Rise a little higher. Have more compassion.
Because we realized we are each other.

And so, when you hurt another, you are literally hurting yourself.
And when you are kind to another, you are helping yourself.
We all were the same energy.

And so, we together, as this energy, wondered or mused or dreamt...
   What might we create together?
      How high can we go?
         How low can we go?
Can we create heaven for each other? Or do we choose hell?

And then I could see in this intense ball of life, of lives, that it wasn't just representative of every human being, it was every animal too. And I wondered how big infinity was!? Whoa! Then every plant and mineral too. Everything that's alive. And it's all alive.

We are each other.
There is no separation.
When we harm, it's ourselves.
When we love, it's ourselves.

And the next morning, when walking down the street, I wondered…
    Was that just me that passed me by?
        Or will I be that flower next?
            And everything was animated
                with the only thing that is.
And the only thing that is
    is us.

ACKNOWLEDGMENTS

Mom and Dad — Gary and Thenell Hanggi, you two wild lovers! I'm left breathless thinking of all the ways you've demonstrated your care for me. The ways you've given. The ways you've shown up. The ways you've let go. The two of you are a masterclass in heart and healing. Your wisdom matches your childlike qualities in equal parts. You have revealed to me my value and my beauty so that I can see it. When I cried to you and told you I was scared you said, "Ask for strength, and then reach out your hand." Thank you for believing that my voice is a gift to others. I will do my best to express my gratitude by sharing what you taught me.

Natalie Roy, you have helped me uncover my own truth. You have taught me how to love difficult emotions because they are a profound gift. You have taught me how to be fearless in my examination of myself, as well as how to accept the parts in me that I want to deny. Thank you for being relentless and insistent that I create this book. I love it when you are bossy — it's such a great look on you! Thank you for making me feel like it was important that I didn't just keep these thoughts hidden on my computer.

Derrick Brown, my longtime pal, thank you for believing in me, encouraging me, opening my mind, and giving me the opportunity to create this book. You are very gentle and loving in the way you guide creatives. It's like you embody the secrets that we might learn in the awkward labor of birthing art. Luna aït Oumeghar, thank you for your beautiful cover artwork and for interpreting the spirit of this book. Winona León, I'm so grateful for your kindness, patience, and talent. Aly Sarafa, you showed me things I couldn't see on my own. I appreciate your clarity! Wess Mongo Jolley — I mean, I just love your name! Thank you for seeing into me, for nurturing me, and for pointing me in the direction to grow. You are more than an editor; you are a wise word wizard! I feel like you took me into your cave for instruction, and like all great teachers, you kept telling me the answer was in my own heart.

Caitlin Sammons, where would I be without your optimism and assurance? I hear that bright voice of yours when I'm afraid. Your light came at the perfect time. Craig McEldowney, you spoke to me in the language of poetry when I needed it. I feel honored that you spent so much time with these early pages, nudging me and supporting me. Your friendship has been key in this creation.

Natalie Avital, John Davisi, Kelly Devine, Scott McLean, MK Lawson, Mikey Rosen, Katie Dalebout, Brent Geisler, Monique Coleman, David Forest — you are the very best friends a woman could wish for. You have loved me and lifted me over and over and over again. Jamie, my dear teacher, who you are keeps working on my soul. To everyone in my tribe that contributed to my growth, who searched alongside me, who have asked the interesting questions — let's never stop!

Jerzy Jung and R. Walt Vincent, you were two of the first people who caught the vision. Your talents helped me unwrap an invaluable piece of the mystery.

Brent French, thank you for your gift of art, for feeling my intention, and interpreting it with your sensitive capacity to feel.

Heather Weiss, you are a star-child and a bad ass! Thanks for jamming with me, for fleshing things out, for being a seeker.

Beth Stine, I am so grateful to hold your hand as we walk down this road together and discover what this road even is.

Laura Davis, thank you for meeting me with such grace and shelter and knowing. I am constantly expanding in the space we create together. Cathleen Moynihan, your compassionate example and thoughtful mentorship led me back to myself. Thank you for showing me a glimpse of the future.

Maddie Corman, my sister, you taught me how to be brave. You showed me that we do it because it's the next right step to take. That we do it out of service. That we do it imperfectly and full of mistakes and anxiety. That we do it by telling our story. That we do it by listening. That we do it because it matters.

Rob Bell, come on!! Are you kidding me!? What kind of wonderful world is it that I get to learn from you? I'm always taking notes. I'm so grateful that you and Kristen have open your arms and your hearts to me. You demonstrate through who you are that "joy is the engine of the Universe."

Jimmer and Michael Hanggi, thank you for being great men. I love your families and I love having you both as my dear friends. I feel like I won the lottery when it came to brothers.

This book was made through the experience of everyone I've had the opportunity of directing and collaborating with, the students that have taught me, those teachers who have guided me and shown me the way, and all those I've healed alongside of.

"We're fascinated by the words, but where we meet is in the silence behind them." — Ram Dass

ABOUT THE AUTHOR

KRISTIN HANGGI is a theatre, television, and film director as well as a passionate multi-hyphenate — writer, producer, creative guide, artist and poet.

She is best known for directing and developing the international smash-hit *Rock of Ages*, which received five Tony Award nominations, including a nomination for Best Direction of a Musical. She has directed productions of *Rock of Ages* all over the world, including Broadway and the West End. Ms. Hanggi developed and directed the acclaimed pop opera *bare*, which ran to sold-out audiences in Los Angeles and off-Broadway, won numerous awards and has gone on to have hundreds of productions internationally.

As a film director, Kristin directed *Naomi & Ely's No Kiss List*, an adaption of Rachel Cohn & David Levithan's popular novel of the same name, starring Victoria Justice. She made her feature directorial debut in 2013 with the indie *Grantham & Rose*. For television, Ms. Hanggi adapted and directed the hit book series, *Dear Dumb Diary* into a musical movie, under Executive Producer Jerry Zucker for Walden Media. She recently directed on a new Netflix musical series.

A partial list of past stage productions include: *Clueless*; *Accidentally Brave*; *Romy and Michele's High School Reunion*; *Atlantis*; *Pirate La Dee Da*; the initial production that launched the Pussycat Dolls, *Pussycat Dolls Live at the Roxy*. Ms. Hanggi graduated with her Masters from USC after receiving her Bachelors from UCLA in Theater. In June of 2013, Kristin returned to her alma mater when she received the UCLA School of Theater, Film, & Television Distinguished Alumni Award. Kristin has a love of music, and has directed multiple music videos and short films. She hosts a weekly podcast with her best friend Natalie Roy called "Let's Play: The CREATE Podcast" on the intersection of spirituality and creativity.

WWW.KRISTINHANGGI.COM

www.ingramcontent.com/pod-product-compliance
Lightning Source LLC
Chambersburg PA
CBHW012106090526
44592CB00019B/2670